THE AUTHOR, PUBLISHER AND ALL AFFILIATED PARTIES ARE NOT RESPONSIBLE OR LIABLE FOR ANY ADVICE, COURSE OF TREATMENT, DIAGNOSIS OR ANY OTHER INFORMATION, SERVICES OR PRODUCTS THAT YOU OBTAIN THROUGH THIS SITE. YOU ARE ENCOURAGED TO CONFER WITH YOUR DOCTOR WITH REGARD TO INFORMATION CONTAINED IN OR THROUGH THIS BOOK. AFTER READING THIS BOOK, YOU ARE ENCOURAGED TO REVIEW THE INFORMATION CAREFULLY WITH YOUR PROFESSIONAL HEALTHCARE PROVIDER.

LIMITATION OF LIABILITY

THE MATERIALS IN THIS BOOK ARE PROVIDED "AS IS" WITHOUT ANY EXPRESS OR IMPLIED WARRANTY OF ANY KIND INCLUDING WARRANTIES OF MERCHANTABILITY, NONINFRINGEMENT OF INTELLECTUAL PROPERTY, OR FITNESS FOR ANY PARTICULAR PURPOSE. IN NO EVENT SHALL OR ITS AGENTS OR OFFICERS BE LIABLE FOR ANY DAMAGES WHATSOEVER (INCLUDING, WITHOUT LIMITATION, DAMAGES FOR LOSS OF PROFITS, BUSINESS INTERRUPTION, LOSS OF INFORMATION, INJURY OR DEATH) ARISING OUT OF THE USE OF OR INABILITY TO USE THE MATERIALS, EVEN IF HAS BEEN ADVISED OF THE POSSIBILITY OF SUCH LOSS OR DAMAGES.

Table of Contents

- Introduction 6
- Overview 9
- Bonding with Your Baby 11
- Talking to Your Baby to Increase Intelligence 13
- Reasons Your Baby Won't Stop Crying 16
- Dealing with Teething 19
- Crib Sleeping Vs. Co-Sleeping 21
- Sleep Training for Your Baby 23
- Learning to Walk 26
- Potty Training 29
- Dealing with Clingy Babies & Separation Anxiety 31
- Formula Vs. Breastfeeding 34
- Introducing Solid Foods 37
- Avoiding Choking & CPR Basics 40
- Keeping Your Baby Safe At Home 42
- Baby Development Timeline & Milestones 45
- Summary 48
- We Want Your Feedback on This Book! 50

Introduction

Let's face it; when it comes to children, we adults whom are expected to take care of them have no idea of the many tough challenges that lies ahead. Yes, you've managed to get some of the best apps for your iPad; it sounds great that you're getting along so well at your work; besides, it's empowering that you've done well in your finances.

However, no smarts will prepare you from the barrage of problems parenting a baby would deliver. Trust me, after only a single day with your precious one, you will be wishing that your child should have come with an instruction manual. That's how I felt too, even before we left the hospital back then. You know why that is? Because the kind of problems you'll encounter are a thousand times more baffling than learning how to use Android the first time. And even if you're managing real people at work, it doesn't mean that you should have all the confidence in the world in having a little person under your wing.

A baby is always a handful. And unless it has only been recently when you last had one, you can never say that you won't get to those awful moments of cluelessness. Most often, you'll be a first time mom. For others, it must have been years already since you last had babies at home. Either ways, this book should lessen the mistakes you are bound to make.

If you are in search of how to make things easier, especially when it's about being a wonderful parent to a baby, this book is filled with treasures. Discovered by real moms, after they've gone through too many trials and errors, you'll be thankful that you had so many topics to warn you of dangers.

In addition, there have been a lot of discoveries the last few years in regards to parenting an infant. For instance, I used to think that letting the baby sleep at hours close to evenings would hinder a good night's sleep. After I've asked some questions to more seasoned mothers though, I found out that babies are different. With them, sleep begets sleep.

Not letting them sleep in certain hours would make them more tired when it's finally bedtime. This actually causes more trouble than good. Tired babies would tend to cry longer before easing to bed eventually. Practices in the past towards baby development, nursing, feeding and a lot more have changed because of tremendous research. Attitudes you have towards those topics may not apply anymore if you haven't read up-to-date parenting books like these.

Expect this book to ease your way in your transition to parenthood. Along that path, you will have plenty of issues. At the same time, you'll determine how things should have been so much easier if you just stumbled into this book before the birth of your baby. If you are already faced with the dilemmas we're talking about, it's still not too late.

This book is well organized so it's simple to glance over an issue that might be troubling you at this moment. It is also written in a no-fuss and devoid of fillers form of writing, which makes it comprehensive in delivering solutions to a lot of issues even in its small package.

"What should I expect the first year?"

Every good mom or parent should be asking this question. From there it drains down to more topics that each leads to a thousand questions. Whether you still have time to prep, or you're already engaged in those daily battles, this book has some of the most significant solutions to real-world mom problems coming from varying perspectives. Having all these solutions in such a compact and accessible book allows a parent to maximize what your bundle of joy has brought – some of the best moments in your life.

Overview

As parents, it is our duty to create a warm and welcoming environment where our bundle of joy can grow safely. We are their main caregiver. Thus, we have to understand what kind of support and experiences we will be providing them as much as we can.

Moreover, it doesn't simply end with us being experts in terms of their health and safety. We also have to introduce them to opportunities that would allow them to explore. Infants are filled with curiosities. Hence, even though most of us parents are learning as we go along, we have to somehow become experts in the few short weeks we have to get ready. Because when the baby does arrive, courtesy of the stork, there's not much time for anything.

Take my case as an example. I could still almost feel the suspense of having to wait for the baby in a span of four more weeks. There are days when I feel like I'm sweating needles. Thankfully, I've always been a "prevention is better than cure" type of person. Because of that attitude, and with the help of my hubby, I've been able to wrap up the shower plans, shopped the entire hospital checklist and painted my baby's nursery ahead of time. My readiness gave me an entire month to soak up all the anxiety my hormones decides to throw at me. This is the point when I decided to start investing in what I should know. Because if you think about it, with all the investments you are more than willing to spend at your pregnancy, baby stuff, room renovation, hospital bills, baby shower etc... most of us still forget how are we going to get around the day-to-day dilemmas ahead. Also, I was advised by all of my mom friends to begin doing research or to start hanging out with them more often. And I'm very thankful in doing that.

To be honest, the advice I got from my mom friends of not worrying too much about labor but instead focus on subjects like baby development milestones, helping your baby learn to talk, formula versus breast feeding, crib sleeping versus co-sleeping and other parenting an infant must-haves is the gift I cherished the most. For me, it has even eclipsed some great items from the baby shower.

Having said that, I too want to give you a gift that would turn out to be much more important than any material things you might get. When you are torn between having to decide whether to call a doctor or not, you'll be much more thankful with the investment you're going to make in purchasing this book.

Ascertain that all babies go through periods when their cries seems impossible to calm. When this happens, not having the correct reactions leads to helplessness and frustration. We have to realize that it's the baby's only form of communication. Thus, it could mean a bunch of different things. That said, you have to familiarize yourself with some of the other clues a good man looks forward to see what the baby is actually trying to say. The trouble is, not all moms worry about the kind of investment it takes to sustain a solution when those future dilemmas come.

Do not leave yourself clueless. This book serves as a handbook or as an instructional guide for the most precious being that will arrive in your life. Educating yourself with the topics contained in this book, would allow you to move more freely, squash some of the worries and remove all impediments that you would have otherwise given your baby.

Bonding with Your Baby

Shortly after delivery, the process of bonding occurs naturally with every mother and baby. A mom is programmed to want to have her baby close to her body. Even at her most fragile state, she will have an unquenchable urge to snug the baby near her, rock the baby gently, sing or talk to the infant as she starts nursing for the first time. It is during this period, when mothers report having a feeling of immense emotions like love, care and tender feelings towards her newborn.

What's almost magic is even without a drop of knowledge of the outside world; a baby instinctively opens his eyes, cries, smiles, latches on to be breastfed the first time, and makes cute noises, which causes the child even more endearing to the mother.

What Makes Bonding So Important For Babies?

The bond that an infant shares with the mom is something that would make an impact to the rest of his life. Next to this is the fathers bond with the child. Together, both the parents should never take for granted the importance of the amount of bonding time they have for their infant. Because it would affect the baby's personality, health, self-confidence, intelligence, relationship with others and ultimately the baby's happiness later on with his life.

According to many studies, infants who are given plenty of positive bonding time by their parents or guardians displays the following:

- Becomes More Independent
- Have Better Relationships

- Scores Better Emotional Intelligence
- Are Team Players
- It Is Easier For Them to Stand Up From Mistakes
- Are Better Communicators Overall
- The "Spoiling" Myth

Contrary to the popular belief of previous generations, attending quickly to a baby's crying doesn't impair their personalities by turning them into spoiled brats. If you are quick on your feet as a parent to hold or nurse the baby the instant you hear him/her crying, the child will not grow up to be a bully as most studies have examined.

I urge every parent, or any primary guardian of an infant to not worry about this myth. You are not doing anything wrong even if you decide to hold on to your baby because he's been fussy all day. It simply implies that you are concerned and you always want what's best for your child. In reality, lots of research has already proven that babies who are comforted immediately during times when they are distressed are more likely to develop the positive benefits we've mentioned above.

All that you're doing is improving the bond you have with the child. Whenever you permit yourself to be touched by those old myths that go contrary to your instincts as a parent, you are actually causing more harm than good. It's because you are acting out of your normal character. And since imitation is the greatest skill a baby initially has, he/she will most likely pick up your "out-of-character" behavior that you displayed.

Talking to Your Baby to Increase Intelligence

A research done in the University of Kansas before the turn of the century is fueling a new debate of another factor that leads to increasing the intelligence of children. The new factor that is being thrown in the mix is talking. It turns out that there is some truth in that old saying, "the more you talk to your baby, the more you increase his intelligence".

The Myth is About to Turn into Fact

The myth of having the child exposed to as much spoken language from the parent as possible, is still currently being subjected to more testing. However, as far as small-scale tests goes, the idea has already exceeded some of the researcher's hopes.

The test are performed by following the lives of 42 families with a newborn child. The researchers visits them once every month recording the parent-child interaction and some other factors related to how communication goes in their homes. During the visits, they record every word that is said by both the parent and the child. After the recordings are collected, they actually get to count the words spoken. They even go as far as determining the tone of how the words are spoken, whether they are positives or negatives. This process went on from 0 to when the child gets to 3 years old. It's safe to say they've gathered a lot of data during that span. However, that's only half the job. The conclusion of the research is only proven after they've waited 6 more years to get back on how the child has progressed.

Research Has Almost Proven It

That's what they did. After careful observation of how the child has developed when he/she is already at the age of 9, they we're able to conclude that those babies whose had more positive talks with their parents at a very early age developed more intelligence later in life. Those children became more sociable, got higher grades in school and continued with having good communication with their parents. In other words, if every parent gave as much effort in talking to their children daily as much as the parents whose children did well in those studies, everyone's children would have received the same benefits of intelligence.

To give you an idea of how much the disparity is between those who performed poorly and those families that got the most out of talking to their children when they were babies, let's look at one data gathered by the researchers. On average, the ones who didn't talked to their babies very much only managed to utter 600 words per hour to their child. In contrast, those who did a better job at parenting, allowed their children to listen to more than 2000 of their words per hour.

While we do know that the conclusion of this research cannot be accepted as a fact yet, mainly because it still needs to be carried out in a larger scale, I for one cannot see any harm in doing what it suggests. For me, half of why I've done it is common sense. I confidently believe that although our child may often fail to follow what we say, they will never fail in mimicking us.

Talking to our babies allows them to have a peek to our own intelligence. Those seemingly insignificant chatter that goes like - "mommy loves you", "does my angel feel hungry?", "mommy is driving honey" does imprint something inside their absorbent minds. It's safe to say that from there, we are able to plant the idea of how the more stable mind of an adult work at a very early age. Hence, their emotional intelligence blossoms much sooner.

Reasons Your Baby Won't Stop Crying

Babies cry – a lot. It's the only reaction they have to certain things and the only means of communication that they know of at this early point in their lives. Babies will cry for a hundred different reasons and as a parent, it is your responsibility to know why your child is crying.

The kind of crying does not even matter; it can be a whimper, a wild tantrum, or crying with sobs and hiccups. One thing is for sure, whenever a baby cries anybody around him would be dismayed. Crying is a sign that your baby wants or needs something, but sometimes, it might mean that something is wrong.

Here are some of the most common reasons why your child won't stop crying:

He Or She Is Hungry – this is the most common reason why babies cry. Inside the womb, babies continuously received food and nutrients via the umbilical cord. Babies have not been known to go hungry in vitro, thus when they are born and the umbilical cord is cut – their food supply suddenly runs out.

At birth, babies need to be fed every 1.5 hours to 2 hours. This is pretty often because their stomachs are so low, it can simply accommodate a few ounces of milk at one time. Moms or dads should expect to hear the baby crying every other hour or two hours to demand for their milk.

Diapers Are Wet Or Soiled – no matter how absorbent or how "dry" diapers claim to be, they can only carry a certain amount of liquid before they start feeling uncomfortable. Babies feel the discomfort too when their diapers are wet or if they have just pooped. Some babies would cry incessantly because there is poop in their diapers.

It's a case to case basis though, but in my experience, they absolutely can't stand it. To be on the safe side, always check the diapers when a baby is crying. In the first months, they tend to poop a lot too, but this becomes less frequent as the infant grows and their tummies can hold more food and liquid.

They Are In Pain – baby colic is one of the main reasons why parents are kept by babies up at night. It can really be painful in adults so imagine what it is like for our little ones. This one can cause really intense bouts of crying for the child. Some of the ways to alleviate colic is by:

- Making the baby burp after every meal to release excess air

- If you bottle feed, you can use bottles that do not induce colic. These are bottles with better airflow and shapes that help the children take in less air when they are feeding.

- There are anti-colic medications that are perfectly safe for children. You must be sure to consult a pediatrician first before giving any medication to a child.

They Want To Be Cuddled – babies have lived within their mother's body for nine months. The womb is very comfortable, silent and safe for your baby. This is something that he or she misses during the first months of his life.

Parents who place their babies in in cribs or have them sleep on separate beds often experience that a child crying stops as soon as he is picked up. The child is looking for human warmth or contact, especially from the mother. A baby is said to recognize the sound of his or her mother's voice because it is the only voice he could hear inside the womb. Talking to the baby in a soothing tone and cuddling him until he calms down always helps.

Dealing with Teething

Teething can be a particularly difficult stage for parents and babies simply because a baby is not yet able to express what he or she is experiencing. The first milk tooth can start to take fire as early as four or five months or as late as six months. My babies started teething early, but I was fortunate enough not to have a very difficult time with it. The scary things about teething are fever and loose bowel movement, but my pediatrician has told me that this happens only in extreme cases.

What I have gone through in my babies are drooling; tendency to bite or chew on anything they can get their hands on; a lot of crying and low-grade fever. There are also some changes in their poop or stool – it tends to be a little weaker than usual, but this is normal and nothing to worry about. It is also normal for your child to feed a little less when he is teething. This is because his gums are inflamed and it is painful to suck or chew. Also. Since teething occurs at different times, it would be better to arm yourself with a few items that would help when your baby is teething.

Teethers (both soft and hard ones)

There are two kinds of teethers that you can buy. The soft ones that look like they are filled with water or gel, and the hard one are made of safe but strong plastic material. You will need both of these to help your baby get through the various stages of teething. When the tooth hasn't erupted yet, you will need the soft teether to help massage your baby's gums and relieve some of the discomfort he is feeling. You can place the soft teether inside the freezer for a few minutes for extra comfort. The cool sensation will relieve pain and discomfort and give your baby something soft to bite on.

The hard teether, on the other hand, is useful once the tooth or teeth have already erupted. You will know that when you see small white bands on your baby's gums. He or she will need something solid to bite on so that the tooth will emerge fully. Rather than have your baby bite on his crib, or in some cases, your arm, better have the baby vent his frustrations on a safe piece of plastic or silicone teether.

Teething Gels

This is my secret weapon when it comes to teething. Applying a teething gel will help minimize the swelling of your baby's gums. This can be readily bought in pharmacies and in baby shops. Baby gels have Xylitol (an ingredient you will also find in chewing gums, I was told), which is a natural anesthetic. It numbs the baby's gums temporarily to alleviate some of the discomfort away. What I do is use the teething gel to my baby's gums before his time to feed. The numbing effect makes him forget the pain and he is able to feed normally.

Teething gels are safe to use, as Xylitol is not a chemical element. Alternatively, you may use kiddie toothpaste as this also contains the said substance. Just remember that the toothpaste must be fluoride-free as fluoride is harmful to children when ingested.

Besides these points, your babies need a lot more patience and comforting for you during this stage in their lives. It would be important to always check for other symptoms such as fever and diarrhea and to bring the child to a doctor should any of the two occur. It would be safer to err on the side of caution if you have small children.

Crib Sleeping Vs. Co-Sleeping

There is a lot of flak against co-sleeping with babies. But the truth is that it is actually better for the child. She will thank you for it when she's a grown-up, and you will congratulate yourself when that happens. However, that will not be something you would be thinking about when you are about to fall asleep with your baby in your arms in bed.

Truth is, it scares me to sleep with a baby in the same bed, whether she's lying beside me or in a crib. She is definitely safer when the crib is at some distance from my bed. However, since I would not be able to catch any sound sleep or continues sleep anyway, then what's the point of her sleeping away from me (granted that it's just half an arm's length away).

Seriously, the books and magazines are correct in pointing out that the best for everyone concerned is to throw the child sleep in a crib, if possible, in another room. More people actually believe that this will instill confidence in the child at an early age. It will also allow the parent – that's me, the mother – to get some sleep. With a separate room, the business of getting back to life before being pregnant starts with some privacy. This is all good and well. For the most part, I agree with this idea, and it has been proven to be reliable.

A parent who does not sleep because of baby distractions will not be able to do as a parent during the day. The mother will be cranky, the beginner will be sluggish, and both of them will miss out on the great experience of parenthood. Besides the real adventure begins when you are able to teach your child new things. Things of importance like reading, computers, sports, and so on…

In a separate room, sleeping in a crib on his own, the baby can have a good rest, in an environment that he/she will treat as her own in a territorial way. She knows that it will be time for feeding because her parent is with him. He/she experiences early on that there is safety even when you're alone.

The other half of the argument seems selfish in comparison. I want my baby beside me because I miss him. I miss looking at him when he's sleeping. He/she is an absolute angel when sleeping. I have better peace of mind when we are sleeping together. Anxiousness doesn't get to me as much because I know that I can comfort my baby the instant he/she cries.

This discussion should be left to pediatricians, child psychologists and sociologists. I am a mom, and I really have no clue if I'm raising my baby the wrong way.

But at the end of the day, or rather at the dawn of the day, I know that I kept an eye on my baby while he's sleeping. I know that we will have better bonding as long as I'm there for my baby the minute I'm needed.

If I'm placing my career on hold because of this child, I will be reading every available minute I receive while I'm sleeping to be beside him.

Years from now, this little quiet time between us will help us to get closer to one another.

Sleep Training for Your Baby

If you're reading after you've given birth and you now have a baby several months old, I know how you feel. You're probably barely able to lift your eyelids. At any moment, you might fall asleep because of the almost nightly ordeal you're going through with the new boss in the house – the baby. I've gone through the same suffering, and I'm sure you're already wishing for a baby whisperer to come knocking in your door right about now.

Fortunately, I've had more than enough experience with those kind of nights myself and so are all of my mom friends. Even before I gave birth, sleep training is already a topic that they're trying to sneak in my head. Because they know how moody my husband is when he doesn't get his sleep.

When I had the time for it a few weeks before giving birth, I joined a couple of mommy group sessions, in which the topic of sleep training was brought out consistently.

From those discussions, I learned that there are two methodologies of sleep training for babies.

First is called "controlled comforting". In this method. A parent trains the baby to try and calm himself by responding to the baby's yearning in longer intervals. Eventually, the theory is that the baby would adopt to the time it takes for his guardian to come to his aid, and that the entire process wouldn't affect the baby negatively that much because it is being done gradually.

The second is called "camping out". In this method, the parent is advised to stay in a visible distance while the baby is put to bed or in a crib. As the child learns to sleep on his own, the guardian then gradually steps back farther away from the child until the time comes that the guardian is no longer in the room.

Both methods are more popularly known throughout the rest of the as the crying it out method. In the US, it is the prevailing method on how to treat a baby when sleep time arrives. Although the same cannot be said for the majority of other culture outside of North America. The latter group protests that doing the crying it out method of making a baby fall asleep is cruel. In fact, a lot of books have already been published to support their indifference.

On the other hand, I personally have found the "camping out" method as what's effective. This came after I've heard the suggestions of all of my mom friends as well. With its help, it didn't take me more than 2 weeks to make my baby sleep for more than 2 hours in the afternoon and throughout the night.

Nevertheless, I will admit that I had my concern on some of the long-term risks that the other camp are claiming in their published writings. I've read a couple. And through my search, I've also stumbled upon more convincing studies about how what I'm practicing doesn't have any ill effects in the development of my baby. I'm talking about an extensive research done in Australia about the efficacy of the "crying it out" method.

In a span of 6 years, they haven't recorded any negative impact that was the result of the sleep training I've practiced. And if you're wondering how extensive the research was, 326 children was observed in the lengthy research. For me, that's more than enough reason. I believe that the fear other parents have is normal, especially since it's obviously another product of the "Spoiling" theory, which was so popular amongst the our previous generation.

Learning to Walk

It's an exciting time for parents when children begin to walk. The sight of a child taking his first steps is pure joy to any parent. Whether this is your first child or your fifth, I guarantee you that you'll have the greatest smile in your face when this happens. This can occur anywhere from 8 to 9 months, to as late as when they are a year and a half old. The age range also differs if you have a boy or a girl. Boys generally start walking earlier than baby girls do, but that is still a case-to-case basis.

Most babies should start to show signs of learning how to walk by around 8 months. He/she will try to stand up and hold on to furniture and take a few steps. Just like anything else, parents must remember that babies have their own pace when it comes to learning to walk. There is no hard and fast rule on when children should learn to walk, or how long the learning period ought to be. As parents, we just have to learn to be patient and keep encouraging the baby to take a few steps at a time each day until he is confident enough to do it on his own.

Here are some helpful learning tool you could use:

Walker or Walking Wings

A walker helps a child his practice balance and standing on his own two feet the first time. This is more helpful than always taking your baby or holding on to him. As with anything, having to experience things on his own makes the learning process easier and quicker for him. With a walker, your baby can take steps without fear of falling down. A word of warning though, children can be exuberant and this means that they should not be allowed in the walker without supervision. Made mostly of plastic materials, these walkers can sometimes tip over and this can leave your baby hurt or injured. When the child is more confident in walking, you can use walking wings to assist him in walking outside the house, in malls or playing in the park.

Protective Gears

When your child is just learning to walk, make sure that he has protective gear on him. In our home, we have the babies wear kneepads or elbow pads made of cloth and plastic. It is also important to baby proof the house once a kid has learned how to walk. Be sure that sharp edges or the corners of tables are properly covered. The last thing you want your child to have a bump whenever he gets up to take a few steps.

Trust

Children who are just learning how to walk are prone to falling and other minor accidents. While you must do your best to prevent these, as parents you must accept these accidents are part of the growing up process. No matter how careful you are at protecting them, it shouldn't reach the point where it is hindering your baby's development. If the baby gets some bruises or slips a few times, as he struggles to stay on his feet, don't panic. You have to learn to let go eventually anyway. Trust your child will find his footing and be able to walk on his own.

Patience

Babies need a lot of patience whenever they are about to complete a milestone. As mentioned earlier, babies learn to walk at different stages in their life and parents should not push or rush their kids until they are good and ready. Rushing your baby may result in injuries or trauma. This may lead them to being more scared and take fewer risks that they normally would have taken. Learn to read cues from your child. He will let you know when he is ready.

Potty Training

There's no need for potty training to be hard, nor should it be stressful for both of you. However, to make the process go smoothly as possible, you have to be well informed if the time is right, and you should be able to attack with a plan.

When is the right time?

Most parent's doesn't try potty training until their child become toddlers, which is usually between the age of 2 and 3. While others tend to wait longer, because they feel that their child has yet to reach the maturity level it takes for this next step in development. Now the question is, "how do we know when our child is ready to face this new challenge?"

Here is a checklist that will tell you what signs should tell you that your child is indeed ready for his next big step towards independence:

Physical Signs

- You can now trust him to walk on his own
- Already has a predictable bowel movements schedule
- Can hold not urinating during naps

Behavioral Signs

- Is able to enjoy watching TV
- Can wear and pull down his own pants

- Has developed a curiosity about what it is one does in a bathroom

Cognitive Signs

- Is able to comprehend instructions
- Can replace his toys where they belong

Now that you're able to distinguish if your child is now ripe for what you want to teach him next, let's move on to the actual training.

Step 1. Make sure that you begin the training by familiarizing him on how to sit on the potty. Set aside 15 minutes of your time in the morning and in the afternoon where you teach your infant how to sit on the potty. The child doesn't have to do anything else.

Step 2. Stickers and an M&M maybe is all it takes to reinforce to a child that what he or she is doing is appropriate. Reward him for every development he makes during potty training sessions.

Step 3. Instruct your baby how it's really done. It's all about consistency and repetition. You'll need a good deal of patience to do this, but the convenience it gives you in the end is well worth it.

Dealing with Clingy Babies & Separation Anxiety

I remember it well. It was when my baby was about 7 months old when she started not even let her daddy hold her. I wouldn't even be able to get off the bed without my baby crying his loudest cry. I would feel angry, not with the child, but at myself. Because I thought, I was doing such a terrible job at being a mother. I was afraid that even with all the learning and preparation I went through before I gave birth, that I still ended up as a terrible mother.

In our previous topic, I noted the importance of bonding time as something that would affect a baby later on with his life. I talked about how the myth of bringing up a "spoiled" person is not true at all and it only originated from theories in the 1920's, which were never actually tested for accuracy through scientific research.

Would you believe it that the same rule applies here as well?

"How is it so?" I'm sure you're asking.

Let's get back to how I found a solution to my problem. What I did of course was to go back to my mom friends and ask for assistance. One of them handed me a book that I missed, which contains information on how to deal when a baby gets to the stage of separation anxiety (AKA the clingy baby stage).

The most important lesson I learned from it is that it is your fault your baby is suffering the stage of being too clingy! However, wait there's more! Although you had 100% to do with it, you shouldn't feel bad about the way you are parenting; it only means that you've done your job well.

The line that I will not forget is that towards a baby's goal of becoming independent, it's normal for children to go through detours along the way. You have to realize that being "clingy" doesn't automatically mean that they'll grow up wanting to be at your side even until they're adults. In fact, displaying empathy is the first thing you have to keep in mind in order to transcend this stage with excellence. They are being "clingy" simply because they really think that you're not coming back and that it's possible for you to leave them. Hence, in order for your child to get pass this phase as fast as possible; you'll have to remove this thought from his mind.

Here are a few things that were suggested to me by my helpful mom friends that I think you should know too:

Slowly leave the room while talking or singing to the baby. It would also help if the baby were currently engaged in something while you're doing this. The baby also must understand that you're about to do something on the side but you're still watching over him. Over time, you'll be able to travel farther and farther without the baby going nuts.

Play peek-a-boo. By playing this game, the child is imprinted with the idea that nothing really bad happens when you're gone. Besides, the way you're laughing and smiling while playing this game gives the baby an idea that you'll return just as fast.

Playing hide and seek. You should play this game if your child develops into this stage at a later age when peek-a-boo no longer is fun for him.

Practice saying bye-bye. Saying bye-bye then going out of sight for a few seconds gives them the same idea as some of the activities I've previously mentioned. Again, it's important that you have a smile in your face upon returning.

Encourage your child to walk away from you. When you're baby is old enough, encouraging him/her to walk towards a play area with other children by himself does a lot to his/her confidence. Stand at a distance and smile every time they look back at you.

Formula Vs. Breastfeeding

This debate has been going on ever since formula milk was first invented. Both sides always manage to present sound arguments to defend their camp. In most countries, breast milk is recommended for infants up to two years old since it is known to contain complete nutrients and anti-bodies that babies need in order to grow strong and healthy.

On the other hand, formula milk is considered a good substitute in cases when the mother is unable to produce breast milk or feed the baby for as often as he desires.

Breast feeding advocates will naturally extol the value of breastfeeding to high heavens. Yes it is great, for these simple reasons:

1. It is totally natural, the mother naturally produces allergen free - breast milk – and so it is free from any unnatural additives that a baby has no use for. There are also hardly any instances of children being allergic to their mother's milk, so this is good for children of all ages, particularly pre-term infants.

2. It is cost - effective – formula milk can be pricey, unlike breast milk that comes totally free and in abundance. For every parent who are trying to cut down on costs, breastfeeding is a viable option.

3. It promotes a bond between mother and child – there is nothing more beautiful than the sight of a mother nursing her baby. Such scenes have been depicted so many times in paintings and sculptures. Although no words are exchanged between mother and child during this period, the emotional bond that is fostered between

the two is carried over for the rest of both their lives, which is irreplaceable than any benefits that can be offered by formula.

Now that we have listed the good points about breast – feeding, it's time to consider the reasons why formula milk remains popular.

1. It is convenient – mix water and the prescribed amount of formula and you're all set. You can feed the baby any time and at any place. It also means that someone other than the mother can feed the baby. Too often, a mom is still exhausted from childbirth and breast-feeding every 2 or so hours. It obviously can take its toll on her health. This is especially true if a mom gave birth via the C-section, which would take days to recover from.

2. It is readily accessible – it is easy to buy formula milk anywhere. In cases where there is inadequate supply of breast milk, formula is used to supplement it. There are times when a mother does not produce the amount that her child needs and so they turn to formula to make sure that the baby does not grow hungry. Working moms do this too, since they are only able to breastfeed when there are at home. Another option that most working moms do is to save their breast milk by collecting some in the morning using a breast pump. When supply is depleted, the mother has no alternative than to substitute formula milk every so often to provide enough nutrition for the baby. This is what is commonly referred to as mixed feeding.

3. They can bottle feed anywhere – society raises an eyebrow on the women who breastfeeds in public. In addition, while we do not agree with this practice, women are often left with no choice but to go with the

flow. Bottlefeeding is the most comfortable alternative when the baby needs to be fed and you are outside of the family, or at a very public place.

Breastfeeding is a decision that is entrusted to the mother. She can breastfeed for a month to six months and then switch to formula if the time comes that she is getting too exhausted. Remember that she is not merely looking after herself, but also her baby, so her well-being matters too.

Introducing Solid Foods

The job of raising a child is hard work. Children are individuals with their own developing personality, unfortunately, first-time parents don't recognize that. It takes parents several years before they get the hang of child-rearing. One of the toughest parts of taking care of a child is the issue of food. This is especially true with the introduction of solid food.

Solid food is a natural progression for babies. There comes a point in time that a baby has to quit drinking milk. Even before that happens, the infant has to start eating solid food. It is easy enough to find baby food in the grocery. But getting her to feed on baby food is not a trivial understanding of the baby.

Solid food can be introduced to a baby's diet as early as four months after birth. But even before solid food is presented to his diet, the child has to be comfortable with different tastes. One way to do that would be to give the baby some natural fruit juice. Most babies welcome the fresh taste experience. Others would latch on to the taste and finish the initial bottle as fast as they can. Some common juices, which babies like, include apple, orange, kiwi and mango. You can either buy these juices of you can squeeze them or otherwise process the fruit to extract the juice.

Babies' drinking juices do not happen overnight. It is important to be patient about this. In most instances, babies will not finish a whole bottle of juice. This is not a problem. Store the juice in the refrigerator and it will keep for several days. If you want it to last longer, keep the juice in the freezer.

As soon as the baby starts biting, you can then introduce mashed apple or some other processed food. Again, there is no need to use store bought processed food. Mashing food for babies is relatively easy. However, if you do not have the time to mash carrots, potatoes, apples and easy, you can start using bottled baby food instead.

During this time, you can also feed your baby with graham crackers, or any soft biscuit. It might take the parents some experimentation as to whether the biscuit would melt in the mouth. Testing for texture and consistency ensures that the baby would not want a particular flavor, in which case, a different flavor would be in order. You might need to rotate three different flavor would be in order. You might need to rotate three different flavors, handy for when your baby wants to have baby food.

A baby may not be able to finish everything that she bites into. You may want to store the rest of the opened baby food in the refrigerator. It is important to follow the manufacturer's instruction on keeping baby food. To keep the baby's dining area clean, there is nothing to do but to feed the baby at a reasonable pace. The baby would be keeping the food in her mouth instead of swallowing it. This is just a stage in the baby's development, and there is no need to fret about this.

Some babies respond well to a regimented schedule for eating, as well as for keeping the high chair clean. While others cannot eat without leaving crumbs all over the place. Whatever style of eating that you baby has, it would be a good idea to teach discipline to the baby. This baby may respond and keep good eating habits, or she may not give a care about the mess she made, what's important is that the baby likes to eat solid foods.

Ultimately, the secret to teaching babies to eat properly is to keep repeating the lesson. This would take a lot of patience. The patience would pay off when your baby joins you at the table eating on his own and unassisted.

Avoiding Choking & CPR Basics

During pregnancy, I had a thousand questions in my mind. One of them is what are the most basic thing that I should never miss to learn as a young mother? I've actually asked several health care providers about that and their responses are usually similar – first aid knowledge on choking and CPR.

However, as I've stated earlier, I'm a firm believer that prevention far outweighs cure. Hence, we'll cover prevention knowledge first before we delve into how to be ready during first aid situation with a choking child.

Avoid High Risk Food – Some foods are harder to consume for a baby than others. And then there are kinds of food that should be avoided at all especially when your child has just recently started to eat solid food. A pediatrician would usually advice you to avoid food that are sticky, tough, and larger than half an inch and slippery round kind of foods. These kinds of foods may not sound any alarm for an adult, and maybe that's why SID (Sudden Infant Death) because of choking still happens. It's easy to overlook these things especially if you have yet to place yourself in the situation your child is in. Consider that even vegetable, which we all know as healthy can easily be stuck in a baby's oesophagus blocking his air passage.

Food preparation has also a lot to do with it. A parent, guardian or any babysitter can significantly reduce the risk of choking by simply cutting the food into smaller bits, softening tough meats by cooking them longer, and supervising your little one so that he doesn't move around while eating.

Choose Toys Carefully – Every toy available these days have a child age recommendation printed on its package, or engraved in its parts somewhere. Before you make any toy purchase for your bundle of joy, always keep a presence of mind to check this recommendation. The age indicated doesn't only come from the manufacturer, but also from governing organizations dedicated in maintaining its intended users safe, which are our babies. Toys meant for infant shouldn't have any removable parts, which can be swallowed by our child.

Firm Bed, Remove Any Unnecessary Things – inside a baby's crib, or the bed where the baby sleeps, should be a firm mattress especially made for babies. Loose bedding, stuff toys and even pillow should be removed. A baby really doesn't need it. And could actually pose more harm than comfort. There has been a lot of research dedicated to figuring out what exactly causes SID, but no one is able to pinpoint the real cause of it. Nevertheless, many believe that placing unnecessary soft items in a place where a baby sleeps greatly increases the chance of clogging.

If you're in a situation when a child is obviously having trouble breathing, you do not have a second to spare and quickly help the child. If there is something stuck in his throat that you can pull out, otherwise if the object is too deep, keep your fingers off the mouth.

Begin to Give the child 5 quick blows in the back. It should be right at the midpoint of the spine between the shoulder plates.

If you're prepared to do CPR then do so, otherwise, stick to chest compression and refrain from breathing into the baby's mouth.

Do not forget that after more than a minute, call 911.

Keeping Your Baby Safe At Home

For first time parents, one of the primary concerns is the safety of their baby, especially in their home. Of course, every time that parent will have a baby, they will give utmost importance to the safety of the environment in order to give them a decent environment to grow in.

If your baby is coming and on his way, there are always tons of things to think about for both parents (especially the mothers). Aside from ensuring that you have the correct kind of baby items, furniture, and clothes for your new daughter or son. You will also like to double check that your house is very secure. Below are some of the useful tips that can provide assistance to parents like you in covering all the safety areas.

First, here are some things to consider before taking your child home

- It is recommended to check the crib, particularly the safety together with other baby items. Several first time parents welcome using "hand-me-down" items from their kin, relatives and friends. This is a very practical approach; however, parents should not compromise safety, as some of the items can be unsafe for the baby. One sure thing that parents can do is about the baby cribs and mattresses – these items should have the approval of strict governing bodies when it comes to safety standards, which mostly can be seen from products coming from the US or Europe. Therefore, if you are to receive a hand-me-down crib, make sure that it complies with a certain standard that you can trust and have not received any news of recalls. You can find this information by visiting the official website of the

US Consumer Product Information Safety Commission. This arrangement can also be contacted by telephone at 800-638-2772

- In the crib, it is important that there are not much clutter of blankets, pillow and even stuffed toys or animals. This is necessary in order to forestall the possibility of suffocation of your child.

- This tip is not only for the newest member of your household, but also for everyone. You have to double check that the smoke and carbon monoxide detectors installed in your home is in safe working condition. There are methods of determining this. It is recommended to put at least a smoke detector on every floor of your home and in the halls located outside of the bedrooms. Being alert is also recommended such as having an escape plan in case of emergency such as fires.

- Place important emergency numbers near every telephone in your house, both wireless and wired phones. The advantage of having a wired phone is that it will operate even when there is no electricity and a cellular phone runs on a battery that has a time limit in emergencies.

- It is important to make sure that your home address number is easily seen so that the rescue squads can easily locate you or get to you as fast as possible in case of emergency

- Also ensure that the handrails in your home are properly installed. It is advisable to always have the handrail when you walk up and down the stairs, particularly when you are carrying a baby in your other arm.

The above points are more helpful for newborns, but how about if your baby begins to crawl or walk? It will only take a few months before your child will begin doing this. In this case, think ahead and provide a secure environment for your toddlers.

- Electrical sockets – cover the sockets using the vent plugs. In the same manner, keep the electrical cords out of reach of your child.

- Part of growing up for babies is exploring. To insure their safety, make sure that furniture are secured in its place so that your baby cannot tumble them over by pulling or pushing.

- When it comes to sharp corners and edges inside your home, place protective padding to make them safer. Safety gates and latches are recommended to be installed wherever there is danger. Keep the cleaning items and materials, most importantly the poisonous ones out of the baby's reach. Small objects are hazardous for your baby look for them and keep them away.

- Consider your water heater, it is recommended to set the temperature setting at most 125°F and temperature above this is dangerous to your child.

Baby Development Timeline & Milestones

There have been studies on the subject, and any first-time expecting mom would most probably read up on babies. The anticipation and excitement does not abate after the child is born. On the contrary, the sense of relief that the baby is going home, at the same time, most women are fascinated by how fragile and helplessness their baby looks. All the same, really, as any grandmother would admit, the adventure is just beginning.

The growth of a child is a personal story and a treasure trove of memories. With the strong emotions involved, and the heightened senses while these moments are happening, these memories are indelible pictures and personal movies that are a joy to recall.

The brightest memories are personal one on one experiences, like the first time the baby latches on her mother's milk, the first time he/she coos, and then afterwards when he/she says that magic word "mama". Other memorable highlights of a child's early years are the first time she stands and her initial steps.

Doctors and academicians would say that these are growth milestones, as if the child was a highway going somewhere, or a project under development. Well, in a way it is true. A baby would not recall these memories, although the mother would.

Babies are not static creatures. They are not toys or dolls, but living persons with personalities of their own. Any mother would know that, the moment she lays eyes on her child. A baby's business is to grow up. She does that by sleeping and eating, and wiggling about.

Before he/she can crawl, he/she need to have the strength to raise his head first. Before the child can walk, he/she would toddle while holding on to a piece of furniture or her crib. Before he/she can call his parents, the baby first grunts, moans and cry.

Endless curiosity and boundless energy impel a baby to grow and grow in small "baby steps". Incremental improvements are not easily detected. Nevertheless, these small steps are preparatory to the great ones.

When your baby takes his first steps, a mom has the pleasure to assist him. Holding her hands tight, and swaying them a bit at the same time so the baby can affect his legs forward at one time. Teaching a child to walk in that manner is backbreaking work, which is quickly forgotten once the infant starts taking steps on his own.

One important thing to remember is that while there may be milestones and timelines set by experts, your baby will grow and achieve these milestones at his own time. Babies are like that. They will not be coerced to do something that they are not ready for.

It can take a few weeks to a few months before your baby starts lifting his head, roll on his stomach, or sit on his own. He/she must achieve these developmental things. But simply because he/she is a little late or early doesn't mean that he/she is not normal.

It is a common misconception that when a child does not follow these timelines, then something is wrong with him. That is not true. It is not a gauge of what your child will be like, rather it is merely a guide for parents to become more observant on how your child does. For instance, if your child was a born pre-term, it is normal for him to lag behind other infants in terms of some of these milestones.

It may take her a while to sit by herself or stand up and utter her first language. She will catch up eventually, especially with his mom's coaxing and help.

Encourage your baby and most of all and enjoy these little victories. These are the medals and trophies that parents keep in their hearts.

Summary

Your life before you were pregnant is gone as you know it. But I mean that in a good way. Because you'll want it to go where your baby needs you to. As a mom, I wish I could tell you that the journey is filled with milk and honey. But, I'm sure you already know that that is not the case. If you've done your homework, you should know some tips and tricks already that would make your life bearable with a newborn. If you've done a good job at research by reading trustworthy resource based on real mom experiences, such as the contents of this book, your experiences would prove better.

The advice that you get should be more than to make life less miserable. It should worth more than that – it should push for wonderful, magical and even fantastic! I can't tell you how many moms I've met that told me "I wish I knew these useful information before my first". Honestly, I've said that line a few times myself. This book is a compilation of the most helpful parenting advice I've learned from more seasoned moms and a few that I've taken myself – unfortunately through trial and error.

I would be lying if I tell you that you wouldn't have to go through those yourself. Because I hope you do. You see, those consequences of discoveries are part of what makes motherhood magical. What this book does is to make sure those experiences doesn't cross over into becoming painful.

If you already experienced the joy of being a mother to a beautiful child, and so this book will surely remind you of a few things as well as afford you the opportunity to learn new tricks. Inside you'll discover new methodologies of feeding and training a child to sleep backed up by extensive research. I've also written substantial studies to bust a few myths that you might still practicing even though they really aren't boosting the progress of your baby.

For us humans, there is always a need to brush up on things that we eventually forget. Surely, you don't plan to rest your parenting skills on what stock knowledge tells you. Doing this is pretty close to being irresponsible, as tremendous studies have been done the past decade or two. Studies that you won't have access to if you're only to rely with friends or family member whom are too only relying on theories that were used-to-be.

If you're looking for a handbook or an instructional manual that should have arrived with your child, then this is book is the closest reference you can use. Listen to actual experts who have identified their most important parenting knowledge into a simple and straightforward format, which you'll want handy often.

A child's job is to break into a toddler and so forth, ours is to make sure we have all the needed ingredients into the mix. This book will serve as the recipe on how you will arrive to that wonderful person you dream of meeting someday – your baby as an adult.

We Want Your Feedback on This Book!

Our main purpose is to make sure that our readers get value from the books we publish and that they have a good experience with all of our products. We are always working to improve our books and other products with every revision and update.

Every piece of feedback makes a difference in this process. And we would appreciate yours as well - whether it is good or bad.

Please take one minute to let us know what you thought by following this link:

http://checkmatemg.com/feedbackbaby/

www.ingramcontent.com/pod-product-compliance
Lightning Source LLC
LaVergne TN
LVHW051756250225
804528LV00002B/319